UNCLE BOBBY'S FINALLY SOBER

BOB LANG

Psalm 30 Publishers

Special thanks to Dave Rolph and Dan Kotoff for their encouragement and help in preparing this book.

UNCLE BOBBY'S FINALLY SOBER
IS AVAILABLE ON AMAZON AND KINDLE BOOKS

EL TIO BOBBY ESTA' FINALMENTE SOBRIO
IS AVAILABLE ON KINDLE BOOKS ONLY

BOB'S CHILDREN'S BOOKS:

THE ADVENTURES OF TYRONE, THE MOTORCYCLE RACING DINOSAUR
IS AVAILABLE ON KINDLE BOOKS ONLY

THE ADVENTURES OF FOUR PUPPIES, ONE WHO WOULDN'T LISTEN
IS AVAILABLE ON KINDLE BOOKS ONLY

Scriptural quotations in this book are taken from the New King James Version of the Bible. Copyright" 1982, Thomas Nelson Publisher.

Uncle Bobby's Finally Sober.
Copyright© 1987 by Bob Lang
Library of Congress Catalog Card Number 87-90448
ISBN 0-9618264-0-1

I dedicate this writing to Judi,
my wife and buddy,
who God through His love
prepared for me.

Contents

Introduction

I loved alcohol from the first swallow on. As a high school junior in Memphis, Tennessee, it was the answer I had been looking for. It tasted terrible, but in minutes after its discovery, I lost my shyness and became the life of the party that I was attending.

In the days that followed, I not only quickly got hooked on the alcohol, but also the applause that I was receiving at parties that I interpreted as acceptance and love. I was starved for both and the price I was paying at the time was cheap for what I thought I was receiving.

What started with my first drink was a romance that lasted nearly twenty five years. A romance that nearly cost me my life. At age forty, after over two hundred arrests and dozens of hospitalizations in psychiatric wards, I was near death.

The shocking part of all this was that three years before the end of my struggle with alcohol, I had accepted Jesus Christ as my personal Savior, but yet I remained in bondage.

At that time in my life I had already tried all of man's answers on how to quit drinking and they hadn't worked. God had a different set of answers for me. Very different, but something was wrong.

I tried praying and nothing was happening. I tried reading the Bible, but I didn't understand what I was reading. I was going to church, but I felt like a stranger.

Even though I was told not to feel guilty because my sins had been forgiven, I was still plagued with guilt. I was told not to have any fears, but yet I was in constant torment knowing that I was going to drink again. And I did many times.

At the point of death, I realized that God had been talking to me all along. It is truly a miracle that I am alive today to tell this story of how God worked in such a special way to free me from the chains of alcohol forever.

1

Hey Look, I'm Over Here

"Lang, are you Guilty or Not Guilty?" I had listened to the charges, one by one, as they had been read, and I knew that they were all true.

My Base Commander was glaring at me in silence. Now it was my turn. I knew as soon as I answered, it would become his decision to sentence me himself or give me a Court Martial, which would result in another trial and much heavier punishment. Once again my story was going to have to be a good one.

On this occasion, I had been arrested for impersonating a Naval Officer. After drinking the better part of one morning, I had gone to the Officer's Club in civilian clothes and signed in. Later that afternoon, I was arrested for being in an unauthorized area, resisting arrest, resisting after arrest, not getting back to my base on time, being intoxicated, and, of course, changing my rank from Airman, which is the same as a Corporal in the Army, to that of an Officer.

It was commented at my trial that I was the first 19 year old Lt. Commander that they had ever seen. The comical part of this, if there is one, is that when I was 19 years old, I could barely pass for 17.

Being in trouble like this was not what I had planned when I first started drinking at high school parties. I was not aware that the choices I made then would cause me such anguish later. As a teenager in Memphis, Tennessee, I had turned my back on God and decided to do it my way.

Even though my parents had taken me to church as a youngster, as soon as I was old enough to quit, I did. Outside of memorizing the 23rd Psalm and learning a lot of Bible stories, my walk with God hadn't gone very far.

I didn't know what I was searching for in my teens, but I wasn't finding it in church. As a junior in high school, I took my first drink and my search was over.

Alcohol was the answer I had been looking for. For the first time ever, my friends were noticing me and I became somebody.

As soon as I sobered up, I was still the old me with a hangover, but for a moment in time, alcohol was my buddy and I had been special. Comparing the happiness of the night with the hangover that followed, the pain had been worth it.

Years later, someone who had known me during those days in Memphis said, "You sure use to be conceited in High School." I was not conceited. I was scared to death to let anyone get close to the real me that I felt was trapped inside.

Whenever I would meet girls in the school hallways, I would freeze up. It was only during my after-school hours when I was drinking that I would come out of my shell.

After finishing high school, I was like many others not knowing which direction to take. I was not ready to go to college, and at that time everybody was being drafted by his 19th birthday.

I knew eventually I would have to serve, so I decided to join the Naval Reserve and, soon after, I requested active duty to avoid going into the Army.

By this time, drinking occupied almost all of my leisure time. I seldom went anywhere or did anything without alcohol as my companion.

During my two years of active duty in the Navy, I would have to stand before this same man at Captain's Mast twelve times. Each time I was brought before him, alcohol had been the real reason why I was there.

I don't remember what all I said at my trial, but I was not given a Court Martial or Brig Time which I should have received. With only two years of drinking behind me, I had already learned that if I made up good stories, I could get out of most of the problems that my drinking was creating.

On this occasion, I could have easily spent several years in the Brig for all that I had done, but instead I walked away with a reduction in rank and two weeks of restriction.

None of the other eleven trips to see my Base Commander even brought about anything close to stern punishment. Not once did I ever receive a Court Martial or even one day of Brig time.

Lying to protect myself had become a natural outgrowth of my drinking problems, and with much practice, I had become good at it.

The last week when I was in the Navy, I was puzzled as I went through the usual separation procedures. I was the only one in my group not being called in for the "Why don't you sign up for some more time in the Navy" talk. The day I left, I found out that my file had NOT RECOMMENDED FOR REENLISTMENT stamped on it in large red letters.

At the time, I remember thinking that I didn't want to sign up again anyway, but I was mad that I didn't get the chance to tell them. I thought to myself, "I should have at least had an opportunity to say, No." I was angry at what was happening to me and I wanted to strike out at somebody or something and all that was available was the Navy, even though it wasn't their fault.

A few days later as I drove away, once again, a civilian, I recalled the time in the Officer's Club. When I had first arrived, I had a few people fooled for awhile and I was someone special. For a short time, my need to be noticed had been satisfied. The occasion had ultimately caused me plenty of grief, but it had been worth it. I grinned as I recalled the Bartender saying, "Yes Sir," to me. Later, he had called the police.

I was going to miss "Ole Stu". He was an electrican on our base, who had been like a dad to a lot of us younger guys. I was also worried about him.

It was a real toss up as to whether he could hold out long enough to retire. Old Stu had only a couple of years left, but his drinking had gotten him close to getting kicked out of the Navy several times.

Many nights, a bunch of us would sit around the table drinking beer and listen to him tell us one war story after another until he passed out.

Sometimes he would drink around the clock. He would hide his empty bottles in his locker and then, before payday, when he was broke, he would drain all of them into one large bottle. He would then usually have enough to last himself for another day or so.

Every three or four months the hospital corpman would have to come get Old Stu and haul him away. Each time after he came back from the hospital, he would be fine for a couple of weeks or so, but then he would start drinking again.

Ole Stu was an alcoholic for sure and I felt sorry for him. I admitted that I was drinking too much, but I was barely over twenty-one years old. Certainly, I was much too young to be an alcoholic like Ole Stu. Besides, I was heading for Chicago now. Things there would be different.

2

Then Came The Explosion

"Get up or I'll shoot," Eddie screamed. Still half asleep, I tried ignoring him which wasn't easy. It was 3 o'clock in the morning when he woke me up and he was weaving back and forth pointing a rifle at my head. "You're going to have a drink with me or I'll blow your head off." As he continued to shout I could hear him cocking his gun.

When I had accepted Eddie's invitation to come to Chicago, I knew it was going to be different, but this was not what I had expected, even from him. I had known him in high school and he had been crazy then, but this was too much. "It's your last chance," he hollered at the top of his lungs. Then came the explosion!

The next morning as we stood on the the roof of our apartment building, I realized how fortunate I had been. The hole where the bullet had come out was six inches wide. Only seconds before Eddie pulled the trigger, he had aimed the rifle at the ceiling.

As we looked at the hole, Eddie shared with me that earlier the day before when he was still sober, he had cleaned the rifle, but did not remember reloading it.

This was my introduction to the Windy City. It should have been a forewarning of things to come. Quickly, I found out that Chicago was a great place to live if you liked to drink, since there were bars on practically every corner. It wasn't long before I had introduced myself to as many of them as I could.

As the first few weeks passed, it became increasingly more difficult for me to stop drinking once I had started. Many times I went out with the intention of only having a couple of drinks, but I would spend hours downing one drink after another. My drinking would usually continue until closing time, and then I would get a six pack to go.

A few months after I arrived in Chicago, I bought a house that was destined to consume most of my spare time for the next two years. It also turned out to be a miserable investment. What I purchased was a "shell", which meant I had bought an unfinished house. By doing this I was suppose to save much of the labor cost by finishing all of the inside myself. The fact that I had no training in construction didn't concern me. Since the outside was completed this sounded like a good idea even with winter approaching.

If I had checked things out thoroughly, I would have found out in advance what problems I was going to encounter. Eddie and his friend Al offered to help me as much as they could, but they didn't have any experience either.

Al's dad Herbert, who was a carpenter, said he would help with the inside walls, doors and flooring. However, catching him sober was difficult.

It was through Herbert that I heard about Larry, who at one time had owned his own business. From what I understood when it came to plumbing, heating, and electrical work, Larry had once been the best. Over the years, his drinking had caused him to lose his business and his family and he now lived in Chicago's skid row.

Larry alternately lived at the Salvation Army when he was sober or slept outside on the streets if he started drinking. Presently, he was living on the streets. Since I was at a total loss in the areas where he could help me, I decided to try to get his help regardless of the circumstances.

My first weekend with my newly-formed work party turned out to be quite an experience. My plans were to get all four of them together and then head out to the house. After I picked up Eddie and Al, I went by to get Herbert, but when we got there, he was hung over and throwing up. I had to wait while he opened a full bottle of wine and drank half of it. Once this was accomplished, we left to pick up Larry. I was very much concerned that this unexpected delay would cause us to miss him.

As we approached the heart of skid row, Herbert was sipping on his wine in the back seat while pointing out left and right turns. Looking around, I was appalled at the sight of such filth and squallor. It was difficult for me to imagine how people could live like this.

We finally approached an empty lot where a deserted building had recently been torn down. The crumbled remains were still scattered about in heaps. Herbert told me to pull over to the curb and stop. All I could think of was that he was going to throw up again. I stopped quickly.

When he got out, to my amazement, he started calling out Larry's name. Almost immediately, I heard another voice coming from a cave-like hole dug underneath the sidewalk, and then out of a pile of emerging newspapers, a head appeared. I had just met Larry.

Larry was in about the same shape that Herbert had been in earlier. Sitting on the sidewalk, they passed the bottle back and forth between them. Several police cars went by while they sat there, but they didn't seem to care. For skid row, this was a way of life.

As Larry lifted the bottle to his lips, I could see festering wine sores the size of half dollars up and down his arms. After months of drinking wine and seldom eating, this was to be expected. I wondered to myself about Ole Stu. I sure hoped he would never get this bad.

That afternoon became what was to be a typical outing with them. By the time Larry was feeling good enough to get started, Herbert was mumbling senselessly. In time, I learned that if I didn't give them anything at all to drink, they would be too sick to work. On the other hand, if they drank too much, they would become useless. A delicate balance between total sobriety and staggering numbness was an ongoing task. I failed often.

I found out that it was best to let them share a small bottle of wine in the morning and then at the end of the day, buy them each whatever they wanted. They always asked for wine. They never asked or implied that they wanted anything more.

On one occasion, I decided that, instead of taking them by the usual liquor store at the end of the day for their wine, that I would get them both a good bottle of whiskey. I purchased it in advance and hid it in the trunk of my car.

When we had finished working that day, I gave both of them their bottle before I took them back to where I had picked them up. I was puzzled why neither of them started drinking right away as they usually did. I later learned that after I had dropped them off, that they had gone to their regular liquor store and exchanged the full bottles of good whiskey for several bottles of their usual cheap wine. What they were looking for was alcohol content and volume. Cheap wine simply gave them the best deal for the money.

As the months went by, it became increasingly more difficult to keep Herbert and Larry in working condition. Many times they would disappear for weeks and I was unable to accomplish anything.

Eventually, this project started costing me more than just my time. Incorporated into the price of the house was an allowance I could use to buy materials to finish the necessary work. By late winter, this fund was completely gone and the house was still not completed.

My only choice was to borrow what I needed by putting a lien against the house. Then came another lien, and then another. I kept using good money to chase a bad investment not willing to admit I had made a foolish mistake.

Depression began to haunt me. The more I got depressed the more I drank. And the more I drank the more I got depressed. I was in a vicious circle not knowing what to do to break it.

I started doing crazy things. One Sunday, I began making sounds like a fire truck. This wasn't too difficult since all I had to do was hang my head out of my car window and imitate the sound of the one that was racing three car lengths in front of me.

It was two o'clock in the afternoon when it had gone by. I pulled in behind it from the side street I was on and started chasing it. The wine that I had been drinking all day gave flavor to the chase. It was the same wine that both Herbert and Larry drank. The firemen on the back of the truck kept waving and shouting at me to stop. Several blocks later when I got to my turn, I waved back and the chase was over.

That night I knew that Al, who had been riding with me, would tell everyone what I had done. Attention-getting insanity of this type began to plague me. At times, I thought I was going crazy.

The months dragged by and became a year. Then another year went by. I finally knew it was time to leave Chicago and try something new. All of my attempts to save the house had failed. Even though I had now completed all of the work on the house, the payments on it, because of the extra liens, made it impossible to handle.

I thought about going to California, but everything was so mixed up and confusing. I didn't know what to do. Finally I decided to go back to Memphis where I had grown up and enroll in college. Maybe if I took a few psychology courses, I could find out who I was and what was going wrong with my life. Yes, that had to be the answer.

3

Because of Destiny

As Dr. Rapp began calling the student's names, I could tell that everyone was trying to answer as clearly and distinctly as they could. This was my first speech class and I also wanted to sound my best.

Nervously I cleared my throat as I awaited my turn. When it finally arrived, I answered, "Here," and my voice broke. Once every five years my voice breaks. Today was the day. When it broke, it just hung there for what seemed like an eternity. As everybody turned and looked, I commented, "Looks like I need this course."

I had decided that while I was in college, I was going to try every possible means I could to find out what was going on inside of me. I had failed in Chicago and I was afraid of failing in college. My insecurities were running wild. My hope was that by signing up for both speech and psychology classes that somehow I could pull myself together.

During the next four years, besides going to

college full time, I also sought out jobs that had a prestigious ring to them. The first two years of college I worked in a supper club as a Host. My third year I was employed at a television studio as a cameraman. And my last year, I worked at a night club where a T.V. series filmed two of their traveling shows. In this way I was no longer just Bob Lang. I became Bob Lang of something important.

During my junior year, I became deeply involved with the drama department. Each week they would present a one act play giving the drama students an ongoing opportunity to put into use what they were learning. If anyone wanted to direct a play or act in one all he had to do was sign up and wait his turn. I put my name on the list to direct a play. When my time came up, I had my choice of whatever play I wanted to direct. I was the only one that year who presented an unknown author. In this case, me.

I had just finished writing a play entitled "Because of Destiny". My competion included plays from such writers as Tennessee Williams, Arthur Miller, and Eugene O'Neil. At the end of the college year when the awards were passed out, my play won "Best Award of the Year". I had beaten some of the most successful writers in the business. That was the good news.

The bad news was that my play was intended to be a tragedy. It was based on events taken right out of my own life. It's purpose was to show the world what a rotten deal I was getting. It had won the award as a situation comedy. Thanks a lot!

Shortly before I graduated, I was asked to be Master of Ceremonies for two variety shows for the Red Cross. I had become well known in the Memphis area because of the jobs I had had and also because of the success of my play. On the surface I had learned to put on a phony smile, and with the help of alcohol, I was managing to fool most of the people I came in contact with. Few people knew that inside I was crying out for help. I had been going to a psychiatrist since my sophomore year.

The second of the two variety shows had gone extremely well. It was at the Naval Base outside of Memphis and the audience had been unbelievable. Between every act, my jokes had brought thunderous roars of laughter. After years of supper clubs and night spots, I was well-equipped with good material. Words could not describe the thrill of being in front of a crowd where you could do no wrong.

I got so excited about what was happening that even with as much material as I had, I began using it up quicker then I had intended. Instead of telling one or two jokes between each act, I was telling three or four and sometimes five.

Two-thirds of the way through the show it became apparent to me that I was rapidly running out of material. When I realized what was happening, I began dashing backstage between acts and grabbing the first person I came to. "Hey, tell me a joke quick!" Much to my delight, this worked rather well. Back on stage I even goofed a few of them up because I didn't get the punch lines right, but by this time the audience was so receptive, they laughed anyway. One joke I told I didn't even understand. They still laughed. When the show was over, I was mobbed by people asking me for autographs and commitments to do more shows.

When I finally left, I was in a state of total elation. It had been one of the greatest moments of my life. I went out the back door to my sports car and put the top down. As I drove into the night, I suddenly was aware that I was all alone and had nowhere to go.

Within minutes, I was sitting in a neighborhood beer joint miles away. No one there knew what I had just done. No one even cared. Something clearly was missing in my life, but I still didn't know what. I had tried everything I could think of, but nothing had worked. By all standards, I should have been thrilled by my accomplishments, but I was empty.

In three months, I would graduate. I fantasized what it would be like to walk out on stage and receive my diploma and then pull out a revolver and shoot myself in sight of the entire graduating class. As one beer after another began to fog my brain, my thoughts changed and I made it through another night.

4

Scalloped Clouds Before
The Scream

When I was asked by the district superintendent if I wanted to teach fifth grade, I smiled and said, "yes". I didn't even know what a fifth grader looked like, but I needed the money. As I listened to him talk to me about the school where I was going to be teaching, I recall my mind drifting off as I began trying to figure out how old fifth graders were.

When June had come, I received my degree and headed to New England. I was a college graduate who didn't even know what I wanted to do. Arriving in Massachusetts, I found jobs extremely scarce. They kept telling me I was over qualified and I really couldn't do too much of anything but talk.

Finally, I got a teaching job in this small school district. My main attraction to them appeared to be that I had no teaching experience and no advanced college credits so they could hire me cheap. In fact, I had made no plans to teach school and I had only taken one class in education.

Eight months later when I awoke on the spring morning of April 12th, I was in a drunken stupor. I had already been fired twice for coming to school too drunk to teach, but both times I had talked them into rehiring me. On this occasion I had been drinking since Friday afternoon and I wanted to make sure I didn't go in drunk again. I staggered down the stairs from the room I was renting and headed to the phone booth on the corner to call my principal.

"Mrs. Stevenson," I said, "I won't be able to come in today, I have the flu". I listened in amazement to her reply. "Bob, you don't have to teach today. It's Sunday".

Later that afternoon, I could barely hear Andy's voice over the roar of his Austin Healey. We had first met several weeks before at a sport's car club and had quickly become good drinking buddies.

After my phone call to Mrs. Stevenson, I had met him and we had been drinking heavily ever since. As we wound through the Massachusetts hills, they got steeper and steeper.

As puffs of scalloped clouds peeked out from between the trees and the wind whistled by, I recall the exhilaration that overtook me. The deepening roar of our sports car separated the hills as Andy pressed the accelerator to the floor.

As the speedometer raced past 100mph, the descent from each and every hill top became more breathtaking than the one before. Soon, our

Austin Healey began to leave the ground. We had begun to play a game called "hill topping".

The painful screech of the tires as they returned to the asphalt seemed to pierce the meadows as we streaked by. Then it happened. I had only glanced away for a second when I heard Andy's scream.

The road had been extremely narrow when we had reached the top of the last hill. It was here that Andy first spotted two cars below completely blocking the road. The drivers of the cars had been going in opposite directions and had stopped to talk with each other. Both cars had been totally hidden from view until the last second. By the time Andy saw them, we were in the air practically coming down on top of them.

Month's later at Andy's trial, his attorney argued, "How could my boys have been speeding? They only left five feet of skid marks."

The impact happened so quickly I didn't have time to put my hands up, and I knocked the windshield out with my face. My nose was broken in three places and my eye brows were gone. When I got to the hospital, it took over one hundred stitches to put my face back together. The cartiledge that extended down from my breast bone had been shoved in when my chest hit the hand grip on the dashboard. Every time I took a breath, it felt as if someone was running a baseball bat through the center of me.

Three days into my hospital stay, I opened the telegram from Mrs. Stevenson. My job was gone.

"Where are my clothes? I've been waiting all

morning." I insisted. The nurse looked astonished when I told her the doctor had released me. I had to get her to crank up my bed all the way because I couldn't sit up by myself. I tried to dress as fast as possible fearing the doctor might return and attempt to stop me. He had been to visit me earlier that morning and had told me I was going to be there for at least two more weeks.

As I went down in the freight elevator to avoid any last minute surprises, I had to hold on to the rail to keep from falling down. My face looked like a peeled orange that had been in a black thread weaving contest. If I moved too quickly, my chest would go into muscle spasms and I would let out a groan that could be heard for at least a block. The few people that did see me when I got into the lobby cringed and looked away. Once outside, I called a cab and went home.

Several weeks later when the swelling had gone down in my face, I took the stitches out myself to avoid going back to my doctor.

The night before I left town, I visited Mrs. Stevenson. She was really a nice lady and had only done what she needed to do when she fired me the third time. She and her husband had invited me to dinner and we all had a beautiful evening together. Just before I drove away, she said if I decided to teach again, she would give me a good recommendation.

School was nearly out and I heard that they were already looking for teachers for the following year in Connecticut. I headed in that direction. The very first place I stopped, I was interviewed and hired on the spot for the upcoming fall.

A few days before classes started, my new school district had a "Back-to-School Boat Cruise" for the entire staff. From the minute the boat pulled away from the dock, the booze poured freely. It was not long before the alcohol and the music began mellowing the painful memories of the past few months.

I met Tom at the beginning of the cruise and we talked a lot. It was easy to tell that he enjoyed his booze as much as I did. He was matching me drink for drink and I was making the most out of a cost-free night.

Well into the night I shared with Tom the truth of what happened the year before. As the cruise was drawing to a close, I asked him a question that I obviously had saved too long. "By the way, Tom, where do you teach?" "I don't," he replied. "I'm the Assistant Superintendent". This near-tragedy actually worked in my favor because during the course of the evening, we had become fairly good friends. Besides, I think he understood the problem. Later that year, Tom saved my job on more than one occasion.

Where I lived had by now become of secondary importance to me. Practically every cent I was now making was being spent keeping my bar bills current. It was four flights up to where my rented room awaited me. To call it cozy would give new meaning to the word. When I wanted to get into my dresser, I had to get on top of the bed and fold my legs under me so I could pull the drawers out. It made little difference, though, because there was little in them.

Since I didn't use the closet at all, I paid the

landlady extra to squeeze a refrigerator into it so I could have something to drink if I woke up in the middle of the night.

The bathroom down the hall was shared by over a dozen people. A small old fashioned tub with legs on it stood in the middle of it. The only thing filthier than the tub itself was the plastic curtain around it that dangled helplessly from broken and well-rusted hooks.

As soon as the curtain got wet, it would begin clinging to anything it touched. Since I didn't want it touching me, my answer for this was a simple one. I didn't use it. This did create somewhat of a problem because the inevitable spattering water from the shower quickly filled the surrounding hollows of the aged and sagging floor.

Within four to five minutes, the water would begin leaking through the ceiling into the apartment below. Many times, as I raced back down the narrow hallway to my room, I heard the hysterical wail of the landlady as she groaned slowly up the stairway in search of the culprit. To my amazement, not once was I ever caught.

At the end of the school year, I knew that this town wasn't working out either and it was time to move. I paid my bar bills and packed my bags. California would give me a brand new start.

5

Another Dead End Street

When I woke up it was mid-afternoon and my head was spinning. As I struggled to my feet, the nightmare of what had happened earlier that day began to reappear. The flashing red light that I had seen in my rearview mirror had belonged to a highway patrolman. After he had stopped me for weaving all over the road, I had been given a choice. Check into a nearby motel or go to jail. He told me that he would be watching and if I tried to leave before I was sober, I would be arrested on the spot.

I couldn't believe that this was happening. Less than two weeks before I had crossed the California State line promising myself that I was going to control my drinking.

After days of driving across the country I had arrived to what I thought was going to be a brand new life. If anyone had seen me entering the state, they would have thought I was a total "crazy". I started singing, laughing and letting out war whoops all at the same time.

I had wanted to come to California for a long time. Now I was here and surely things were going to change for me. I didn't know anybody and no one knew me or my past. As I entered the state, I decided right then and there that I was going to become a new person. With plenty of will power I knew I could do it.

Everything I owned was in the back seat of my old clunker Chevy. It was minus one fender that I had knocked off in Connecticut a month before I had left. All I had was five hundred dollars in my pocket, but I didn't care. I was determined that I was going to make it and that things were going to be all right.

Within a week after arriving, I found my third teaching job in as many years. It was almost the middle of August and my 30th birthday was only a few days away. I decided to drive up the coast from Southern California to San Jose where my sister was living. I hadn't seen her in years. She had been married, then divorced and she was living with her two daughters. They were three and five years old and I had never seen either of them.

I had always thought that if someday I got married, I would want boys, but within minutes after meeting my two nieces, they sold me on the idea that little girls are special. They soon became like daughters to me. As it would turn out, they both would be teenagers before they ever saw their Uncle Bobby finally sober.

During my stay with my sister, I had been drinking steadily. The morning my visit was over, I left her house and stopped to have a few drinks. The next thing I remember was the red light in my rearview mirror and the highway patrolman.

Looking at my watch, I knew that I had been at the motel for less then two hours. I peered out the window frantically hoping to see a liquor store somewhere in sight. There was none. I knew I had to get myself sober, but right now I was sick and I desperately needed another drink. I didn't have to dress because I had passed out, clothes and all, on top of the bed. Somehow I managed to make it to my car and drive to the first bar I saw.

Once there, I resumed my drinking until I didn't hurt anymore. How I got back to Southern California I don't remember. I was blacked out most of the way. I vaguely recall a few gas stations and lots of bars and beer joints. The last two hundred miles or so I don't remember at all. Once I arrived, I had two days left before I had to report for work. My promise to myself to control my drinking had clearly been broken. All the will power I had seemed to go right out the window as soon as that first drink went down.

As the school year began, I tried again and again to control my drinking, but everytime I failed. I gave it my best, but it still didn't work. If I drank at night, the next morning I would drink again. Despite this, I was managing to make it to school and teach even though most of the time I was either half drunk or hung over. The days when I was in terrible shape, I would call in sick.

I soon became a regular morning visitor to a

neighbor bar only a half block from where I lived. After a particularly heavy drinking weekend, I found myself standing outside of it early one Monday morning.

I knew it would open at six o'clock and I had only two minutes to go. Watching the second hand on my watch go around was sheer torment. It was barely moving. I could hear the morning bartender inside clinking glasses as he prepared for the day.

It was all I could do to keep from throwing up. I thought if I could only get a few Bloody Marys into me, I could make it to work. I had been absent too often lately and I wanted to show up if I could. My fifth grade kids were waiting for me.

When I got inside, the bartender knew exactly what I wanted. "Here you go," he said with a grin as he placed two Bloody Marys in front of me.

When I arrived early in the mornings, I usually would throw my first drink up and sometimes even the second one so I wanted to be prepared. It made no difference to me. I had long since accepted the fact that this was going to happen. My goal was to keep whatever I could in my stomach as long as I could. This way, the alcohol from the drink would begin to soak into my system and I would start feeling better. In an hour or so, my hangover would start going away.

After a half dozen Bloody Marys and with just enough time to make it to school, I waved goodby. "See you at lunch," he mumbled as he tossed me an understanding wave. He knew I would be back. So did I. Today I was hurting.

Somehow, I struggled through the morning. As soon as lunch came, I headed back for more Bloody Marys. I downed four or five of them in fifteen minutes and then switched to whiskey. By the time I left to head back to school, it was clear I had overdone it. I was a mess.

Even though I had made this same trip dozens of times and knew exactly which way to go, I decided to take a short cut. Looking at my watch, I was aware that the lunch bell had rung at least ten minutes ago. By now, my kids were probably the only line still waiting for their teacher.

"I can't believe this," I screamed hysterically. "Another dead end street." Again and again, I whirled the car around squealing tires as I floorboarded it in a different direction. "Maybe this way," I thought. "If I only hadn't stayed so long." My brain was foggy and I am sure my driving was showing it. Everything was getting fuzzier by the moment.

Finally, I roared into the school parking lot and jammed on the brakes. Screeching to a halt, I jumped out and ran to where my kids were supposed to be lined up. Even though I was over half an hour late, they were still there.

Knowing I was in a stupor, I waved them out towards the softball field. They were used to this because I had done this with them several times before. I tossed the room keys to one of my kids to get the bats and balls and started jogging toward the field.

I looked over my shoulder to make sure they were all coming and I couldn't believe my eyes.

Heading directly toward me was someone in a blue uniform. Panic stricken, I realized that I had been followed into the parking lot and I was about to be arrested right in front of my kids. This was going to be the payoff to a great day. I should have called in sick.

Trying to avoid arrest as long as possible I shrieked at the kids, "Let's run a lap before we start the game." They willingly began trotting along behind me toward the other end of the field.

My mind whirled as I stalled for time trying to get myself together. Finishing the first lap, I hollered, "Let's go for another." I heard a few moans, but most of the kids faithfully jogged on. By now, I wasn't feeling too good either.

I knew as soon as I stopped, it would be all over. I began visualizing my being handcuffed and driven off. I could see the principal standing there with my kids trying to explain to them what was going on.

Only days before, I had received my Life Teaching Credential in California. By now, I was on my third lap and my kids were beginning to drop all over the place. My cry to them to go for lap three had met with considerably more moans than lap two and several collapsed on the spot.

As I continued jogging an ever-increasing trail of kids began dropping on the field behind me. It became quite a sight to witness.

As expected, a faithful few remained with me and were determined to keep up no matter what. Entering my fourth or perhaps my fifth lap, my head was throbbing so badly I knew I couldn't continue. As I rounded the bend the blue uniform was still there and sensing I was about to stop, he started walking toward me.

Realizing it was all over, I angled in his direction resigned to get it over with as soon as possible. As I got closer I noticed he was holding something in his hand. I'll never forget his first words as we came face to face. "Congratulations, Bob." He was a fireman and he was delivering our awards for fire safety.

At the end of the school year I decided to resign and move further south in California to Orange County. I had heard it was a great place to live with a lot to do. Perhaps, I thought, if I kept myself busier I would have less time to drink.

Yes, Jesus Loves Me

Trembling both inside and out I began wiping the steering wheel with a wet cloth. I had to make sure all evidence of my ever having been in this car was gone.

Two days before I had borrowed it from a friend only to beg him several hours later to call it in stolen. I had hit another car and spun it around several times. I was so drunk that I had never seen it coming and when I had stopped, the other driver insisted on calling the police.

Knowing that I would be arrested for drunk driving as soon as they arrived, I became panic stricken and drove off leaving the scene of the accident. My foggy thinking gave me hope that since I didn't own the car, perhaps the police couldn't trace me to it.

Now with my head somewhat clearer, I had returned to the shopping center where I had abandoned it. In a cold sweat I peered through the windshield watching the early evening shoppers come and go. The excitement from their nervous chatter seemed to penetrate the night.

Frantically, I wondered if the police had already located the car and were watching me even now. I rubbed desperately trying to make sure I didn't miss even the smallest area where my finger prints might be found.

To add to my troubles, earlier that same afternoon, I had hung up the telephone with my new school district. They had sent me home the week before for coming back from lunch too drunk to teach. There had been quite scene. They told me that no way would they hire me back. My job was gone.

In a few days, my mom and dad were flying out from Memphis to visit me. In their last letter they had told me that they were really proud of me now that I had quit drinking for good.

All my efforts to avoid detection that night were to no avail, because within days, the police had uncovered evidence linking me with the car. A warrant was issued for my arrest and I was formally charged with hit and run driving.

Several months later when I appeared in court, the other driver testified that I was clearly under the influence of alcohol when I had run into his car. By the end of the trial, enough testimony and evidence had been presented to convince the jury that I had left the scene of the accident because I was afraid of being arrested for drunk driving. When the guilty verdict came back, the judge gave me a choice. Attend Alcoholics Anonymous meetings three times a week for a year or spend six months in jail.

I certainly didn't think I needed A.A. but I decided it was clearly the better of the two choices. I thought to myself that even though I had to go to these meetings, I didn't have to listen. Fortunately, this was impossible. Even as stubborn and hard-headed as I was at the time, I couldn't sit in an A.A. meeting for an hour and a half and not hear something.

Time and again I heard someone relating stories about what had happened to them and how it used to be. I also heard about how it was now. I began to learn all about what was happening to me from others who understood exactly what I was going through. They hadn't found these answers in school. They had lived them.

By the time I got to A.A., I had already been to five psychiatrists, but nowhere had I heard what was being revealed to me through the A.A. program. Much of it I didn't want to hear, but yet I found myself eagerly listening.

My past history seemed to fall directly in line with many of those attending these meetings. Denying that I had a problem, moving from place to place, searching for new beginnings and trying to use will power were all commonplace for people having problems with alcohol.

My first few meetings were full of surprises. First, I had expected to see sour faces on everybody since they couldn't drink anymore, but most of those I met laughed and joked about how great it was to be finally free from all the problems that alcohol had caused them.

I was also very much surprised at the types of people who were attending. I had thought for years that I was too smart to be an alcoholic, but yet I found myself in the midst of medical doctors, college professors, and attorneys.

Another surprise was how many of those I met were still teen-agers. Many were in their early teens.

It wasn't long before I realized that I was an alcoholic and began openly admitting it. However, knowing you are an alcoholic and wanting to quit drinking are two different things. I didn't like the problems that drinking had caused me, but it was difficult for me to accept the thinking that I would have to spend the rest of my life without alcohol.

Something else also began to trouble me. I kept hearing that I needed to turn my life and my will over to a higher power as I understood it. One night at a meeting, I flashed back to my childhood and my Sunday School days and I knew for me that higher power meant God.

I recalled one early Spring morning many years ago sitting on the edge of a crystal clear lake singing praise songs to the Lord. It was the first morning of a church camp and when we had arrived at the lake, the sun was barely breaking between the trees from across the way. We were bundled up from head to toe and the brisk dawn air seemed to crackle as our young voices sang out. "Yes, Jesus loves me. Yes, Jesus loves me. For the Bible tells me so."

That night I flashed back several times to other similar occasions and I knew I needed

Jesus as my higher power, but yet, even as I sat there, Something told me I would drink again.

As I was getting my court card signed at the end of the meeting, someone said, "Keep coming back." Heading to my car I recall mumbling something under my breath about not having a real choice. Even though my year of A.A. meetings still had a long way to go, I was already beginning to count my remaining time.

In the weeks that followed, quite a few of the A.A. members who had gained sobriety took time to talk with me and I sensed they really cared. If I wanted help, they would give it to me. But they made it clear that I had to want it. I knew I couldn't con them. Admitting that I was an alcoholic was only the first step in A.A.'s twelve step program. Through their experiences, they could quickly tell who was ready to quit drinking and who was not.

When fall came I secured a new teaching job only days before the school year started. This was my fifth school district in eight years of teaching. They hired me knowing that I was an alcoholic, but they were content with the fact that I had admitted it and was attending A.A. meetings. I didn't mention to them anything about my trip to court.

Being back to work was a great relief, but I was having a desperate struggle inside of me. I knew that if I started drinking, the chances were extremely good that I would end up drinking for several days. If this happened, then, without a doubt, I would miss one of my A.A. meetings and stand the chance of violating my probation which meant going to jail. I was also afraid of getting into trouble with my new school district. Yet, I wanted to drink.

I had no doubts anymore that I was an alcoholic, but something inside of me started convincing me that if I was more careful as to when and where I drank that I could avoid any future problems. There had to be a way for me to drink and not get into trouble.

Believing this, many ideas ran through my mind. Perhaps, I thought, if I only drank at home then I couldn't get arrested for drunk driving and if I kept a good supply of alcohol in the house, then I would have little chance of even being arrested for drunk in public.

As a teacher, I had several long holidays and if I planned it right, I could drink and still have plenty of time to sober up before I had to go back to work. Then a new thought crossed my mind. What if, when I was drinking, I was nowhere near where I lived or taught? Maybe even out of the country. Then even if I got into trouble, no one would know.

By Thanksgiving, I had been sober nearly six months, which was the longest time I had ever been without a drink in my entire adult life. Once before, I had held out for slightly more than two months but six months was a record for me. I hadn't missed a single day of teaching all year.

My probation officer was so pleased with my progress that at the end of eight months, he recommended that I be released from the remaining four months of my one year sentence to A.A. meetings.

I was elated about this because the Christmas Vacation was only a few days away and I didn't want to be tied down to a bunch of meetings. Besides, I had a trip planned.

The day I received my probation officers letter containing my release, I had just returned from a two week Christmas vacation in Mexico City where no one knew me. Before I left, I had bought a fifth of whiskey and taped a twenty dollar bill to it. I had then placed it on a shelf in my closet.

As I left on the bus heading across the border, I knew that when I got back from Mexico, I would be heading straight to that closet.

When I returned to Southern California, I had been drinking ever since the second day of the trip and it was obvious. I used the twenty dollar bill to pay the cab driver who drove me home from the bus station and then I drank the fifth of whiskey without ever leaving the house.

When it was time for me to start teaching again in January, I had dried out and was ready. No one knew I had been drunk for two weeks. I thought to myself, my plan was working. If I was careful, I could hide my drinking.

However, in the back of my mind, I couldn't forget my trip to court. It had been a scary one since I couldn't stand the thought of having to spend time in jail.

I decided that it would be a good idea to ask around and get the name of a good attorney just in case someday in the future I might need one quickly.

I didn't know it then, but the price I was going

to have to pay for the drinking I was yet to do was going to be much more expensive. In the years to come, the attorney's phone number I received would ring many times.

7

Leaves For My Pillow

As the attendants were strapping me into the strait jacket, my only thought was that if I inhaled deeply and held my breath, I would later have room to work free.

Several years had now passed since my trip to Mexico City. The only reason I was ever sober now was because of the fear of what would happen to me once I started drinking.

By now I was clearly a binge drinker with my episodes quite often lasting several weeks. The end result was almost always the same with multiple trips to jails and hospitals.

I had also begun to go into delirium tremens at the end of most of these binges. The best way to describe the D.T.'s, as they are called, is to visualize wide awake nightmares. Once they start, the mind begins to tumble as if watching several old time horror movies all at the same time. Everything that is flashing before your mind appears to be real and the only solution seems to be to run as fast as you can in order to get away.

Once this condition takes place, unless medical attention is received quickly, approximately one in every four people will die of a heart attack. Consequently, being tied to hospital beds was now a recurring part of this hideous cycle. In addition, permanent numbness was beginning to affect both of my hands.

As they hooked my strait jacket to the bed and began to leave the room, I lied to them and told them I was cold and needed a blanket. I knew that if I was going to try and escape, I would have to hide what I was doing. From the best I can remember, it took me several hours to completely loosen all the buckles and straps.

Lying there under the blanket and now free from my strait jacket, I could see through my partially opened door into the outer corridor. There was only one locked door between me and freedom. After what seemed like an eternity, I finally heard the click of the lock, and the door swung open. Thinking back to that night, I can still hear the screams of the attendants as they chased me.

I ran down seven flights of stairs out into the middle of the night. It was four o'clock in the morning, and it was cold. All I had on was a pair of short pants, a short-sleeved shirt, and sandals, but I was free.

As I stood by the side of the road several blocks from the hospital trying to decide what to do, I recalled the events of the past few weeks.

A close friend had put me on a plane going

back to Memphis. He had tried letting me stay with him for a few days hoping that he could help me sober up. Each day, as soon as he left for work, I would start drinking again. Realizing his plan was not working and not knowing what else to do, he decided to buy me a ticket home. When I arrived at the airport to board the flight, I was half drunk and half hung over.

It was early October and I had lost my teaching job because I didn't report to work in September. I was on a drinking binge that I couldn't stop. A few weeks before, I had been arrested for drunk driving and my brand new car had been impounded. I hadn't made my August or September payments, and when the finance company checked up on me and found out from the school district that I was no longer working, they repossessed my car while I was still in jail.

Before moving in with my friend, I had been living in a drunken stupor in a local hotel running my credit cards far past their limits. Moving from the hotel to his house had only helped me prolong my drinking.

As I got on the plane, my friend told the stewardess, "Please don't give him anything to drink." She had agreed. Minutes into the flight, I had talked her into serving me anyway.

As I sipped on one martini after another trying to get myself together, I noticed a young man sitting two seats across from me by the window. From time to time our eyes would make contact and he would smile. He had such a look of contentment on his face that it made me feel uneasy.

Several martinis later we started to talk and he began to share Jesus with me. I found out that Tommy was an evangelist who was going to be preaching the next morning in Memphis where I was heading.

As we talked, I felt drawn to what he was sharing. At first I couldn't understand how Jesus could possibly love me in the shape I was in. I was a failure. Nobody loved me. Least of all myself. In fact, I had come close to suicide several times in the past few weeks.

Tommy explained to me how Jesus separates the person from what the person is doing. He said that Jesus could love me and yet at the very same time could hate the life I was living. He went on to say that I didn't have to change my life before I came to Jesus. All I had to do was let Jesus into my life and then, through His help, I could change.

Inside of my head I could almost hear the song I had once heard at a Billy Graham Crusade, "Just As I Am". I wondered if that could possibly include me. The more Tommy shared with me, the more I listened.

When we arrived in Memphis, my dad was waiting for me and the pastor of the church where Tommy was going to be preaching the next day was waiting for him. The four of us talked for awhile and then both my dad and I were invited to the service, the next morning. We accepted the invitation. There was no doubt in my mind. I wanted to go. The next morning at the end of the service, Tommy gave an altar call. Without hesitation, I went down the aisle and accepted

Jesus as my Savior.

A few days later when I got back to California, I was flying high on cloud nine. Within a couple of weeks, however, I realized that I was in big trouble. I had accepted Jesus as my Savior, but I was struggling terribly. I had been told to pray, read the Bible, and go to church, but something was wrong.

Even though I was praying, nothing seemed to be happening. I wasn't sure what to pray for or even how to pray. I started reading the Bible, but I didn't feel I was getting anywhere. Most of the time I wasn't even sure what I was reading.

I started going to church, but I felt like everyone was staring at me and I didn't belong. Most of the people I saw my age were married with kids. I pictured them with a white picket fence around their yard and a Cocker Spaniel digging in their flower beds. I didn't fit in at all. As soon as most services were over, I would head straight for the door.

I also couldn't understand why I was having so many problems. I had believed that once I became a Christian, my life would run smoothly. This made me start questioning whether or not I really was a Christian. I began to think that maybe what had happened the morning of the altar call hadn't worked.

In the weeks that followed, I began worrying that I might drink again. Something inside of kept saying, "Maybe one more time." I became mixed up and confused.

My thoughts drifted hopelessly in the direction of drinking again. And then, one night about six weeks after I had accepted Jesus as my Savior, it happened. I took that first drink.

Several weeks of binge drinking followed with many arrests. Now here I was shivering at the side of the road with only moments having passed since escaping from a hospital strait jacket. I had escaped from man, but once again, alcohol had me tightly in it's grips.

My problems with drinking now became even worse than before because I thought that, besides losing everything else, I had also lost my salvation. I believed that I had my big chance and I had blown it. Now it was too late.

The torture-filled days became weeks, then months, and every time I started drinking, the end result was predictable. If I had a job, I would get fired. I would then get kicked out of where I was renting. If I had a car, it would be towed in, most of the time wrecked, and I always could expect multiple court dates for either drunk in public or driving under the influence of alcohol. My failures to appear in court multiplied endlessly. Most of the time I didn't even remember that I had a court date. I had warrants out for my arrest almost all the time.

Even though all this was happening to me, I still continued to drink. It seemed that for years, no matter how many problems my drinking created, as soon as I sobered up, I could straighten them all out. I was once asked what my biggest problem was when it came to my stopping drinking. Without much thought I commented, "My ability to recover."

For years I had made a joke out of the old

cliche, "You can fool some of the people some of the time, but you can't fool all of the people all of the time." I had changed this saying to, "You can fool some of the people some of the time and do just fine." This thinking is what I had lived by.

However, as the months went by, now it was becoming apparent to me that I wasn't fooling anybody anymore any of the time. For the first time in my life, I couldn't get my jobs back after I lost them.

I was renting rooms by the week and, often, by the day in the poorest sections of town, if I could afford them at all. Many nights I slept in my car if I had one. When I had a car it was usually only one sputter away from the junk yard. My past was beginning to catch up with me in a dramatic way.

One day after a courtroom appearance, my attorney stopped me outside as we were leaving. For a moment, he just looked at me and I could see a real sadness in his eyes. I wasn't prepared for what he was about to tell me.

"Bob, when we have court appearances, you're too drunk to show up and I have to get your case continued. I've defended you seven times for drunk driving. The last five, in less then two years. You've had more drunk in public charges than I can count. I'm not helping you and I need to sleep at night. I've decided never to defend you again. Today, we faced our last judge together."

I couldn't believe my ears. I was shocked and extremely angry. He was the main reason that I had spent so little time in jail and now he was telling me I was on my own.

My response to this new crisis was to leave the area and go somewhere that the police didn't know me. My car was gone, so my thinking was that at least I wouldn't have to worry about getting arrested for drunk driving.

It was then that I learned how to survive on the streets. Still making up stories for the occasion, I began panhandling in order to keep myself in cheap wine.

Quite often at night, I had nowhere to stay so I would have to find some bushes to crawl under.

That way I could hide myself until the sun came up. One night before I went to sleep, I thought back to a certain morning in Chicago. It had been a long time ago when Larry had crawled out from under the sidewalk all wrapped in newspapers in order to keep warm. I wondered how he was.

My thoughts continued as I pictured the last time I had seen Ole Stu. I used to feel sorry for them both. I never thought it could happen, but I was just like them now.

I tipped my bottle to my lips and finished drinking what little wine remained in it. I noticed my arms. At least there weren't any wine sores on them. I shoveled the leaves with my hand to make a pillow. I hoped I could sleep until morning.

A Way Of Escape

Thoughts, one after another, raced wildly through my mind stopping only long enough to further blurr the already rambled confusion going on inside of my head. I knew the symptoms, I was on the verge of going into delirium tremens. It could happen at any second and then once again I would have to be tied down.

The doctor spoke softly as he gave me the injection, "Your body can't take the abuse you're giving it. If you continue drinking the way you have been, the chances are extremely good that you are going to die very soon."

The pounding of my heart had inceased to the point where I felt as if my chest would explode at any moment. I prayed that the medication would work quickly. It was my first prayer in a long time.

I had been found wandering the streets in a drunken stupor early one morning and brought to a de-tox house to dry out. Shortly afterwards they had rushed me to this alcoholic crisis center for emergency treatment.

In His love for me, God had let me continue to make the choices I wanted to make even after having accepted His Son, Jesus, as my Savior. Each time I had chosen to drink, I had come closer to death.

As the sedation began working, my mind slowed down and settled onto a letter I had received a long time ago. "Bob, don't let the devil do anything to upset what God is doing for you, because I can assure you that he will try."

This had been Tommy's warning to me shortly after I accepted Jesus into my life. At the time I didn't realize how vulnerable I was and I had discounted this young evangelist's warning. Besides, I thought, I was saved. How could Satan possibly get me now? Within 72 hours after receiving Tommy's letter, I was staggering drunk.

As I lay there, it was hard to believe that over three years had passed since then. I was now 40 years old and it had only been by the grace of God that I had managed to survive the torture that I had been putting myself through.

My thoughts drifted back over the last several years and I slowly came to grips with what had taken place since my first becoming a Believer. Satan actually had two battles with me. His first battle was to keep me from accepting Jesus. After he had lost that struggle, his next task was to keep me, as a new Believer, as ineffective as he possibly could. It was in this second area that he had been most successful.

My pride and stubborness had blocked the

path for God's will to be done in my life. Growth for me had been impossible because I had insisted on running my life just as I did before I accepted Jesus. It was inevitable that I would drink again.

Once that happened, Satan had me right where he wanted me. He then attacked me full speed ahead with guilt and thoughts like these plagued my mind. "How can God love you now after what you've done?" "God was counting on you, and you let Him down." "What a disappointment you are to Him. What's the use?" "You had your big chance and you blew it. Why not give up?" And I did!

Despite the fact that I was drinking again, God did not desert me but instead began dealing with me in a very special way. As a caring Father He couldn't tolerate my wrong behavior without responding, and He had done this by not protecting me from the trouble my drinking was causing.

Many times, as I was about to be arrested, I prayed, "Oh God help me!" As I was being driven to jail, I thought that my prayers were not being answered, when indeed they were. God was helping me, even though it wasn't the type of help I wanted. He helped me by letting the end result of my drinking binges get so painful that I had to quit. That's why I was here right now.

It became clear to me that all this time, even though I had been a Believer, I had never grown up. Staying sober for me was going to have to be more than putting the cork in the bottle, and then toughing it out. I had tried that too many times and it had never worked. Without a doubt, I had to do something different so that running to a bottle for answers no longer made sense.

When I left the alcohol crisis center, I knew that if I ever drank again, it was very possible that I would be signing my own death warrant. Alcohol truly had carried me as far toward destroying myself as I wanted to go.

In my heart I was aware that God was giving me another chance to get my life right with Him and I wanted to take it. As I began reaching out for God's help, each discovery I made seemed to draw me closer to Him.

I found out that even though I had been drinking all this time, it didn't mean that God no longer loved me. Certainly, what I had been doing was displeasing to Him, but He was always there waiting to forgive me. This tremendous forgiveness is promised in His Word. *"If we confess our sins, He is faithful and just to forgive us our sins and to cleanse us from all unrighteousness."* I John 1:9.

I found out that I had to come to grips with what repentance really means. Repentance was more then my saying I'm sorry. I also had to bring about changes in my life so that I wouldn't have to say I was sorry again.

It was here where I had run into difficulties before. I had been sincerely sorry for what I had done, but I still had wanted to do things my way. This had doomed me for failure. Me against Satan had been no match. I had needed God's help, but had been unwilling to let Him help me.

With prayer, reading the Bible, and fellow-shipping with other Believers, God had given me three of the most powerful tools imaginable to insure my growth, but in the past I had only made vague attempts to use them. There was no doubt that this was an area where I needed to bring about major changes. A lot of people were willing to help me understand how to use God's tools, but I had to be open to listening to what they had to say.

When I first heard I Corinthians 10:13, I was amazed at what I had found out. This scripture reveals that, *"No temptation has overtaken you except such as is common to man; but God is faithful, who will not allow you to be tempted beyond what you are able, but with the temptation will also make the way of escape, that you may be able to bear it."*

Here in God's Word I was being told that many other Believers shared in common with me the temptation of alcohol. I was also told that God would not let this temptation get so bad that I couldn't handle it with His help.

In addition, He further promised me a means of escape from my ongoing need to drink, if I wanted it. I had long since concluded that I was trapped within myself with no means of escape. I had come to believe that no one ever had my set of problems before and that's why I drank.

How wrong I had been! I wasn't alone and, with God's help, I could break away from the bondage that alcohol had held me in for so long. God loved me and He wanted me free.

A short time later I came across Romans 8:37 and this scripture became one of the keys to my recovery. It says, "We are more than conquerors through Christ who loved us." It finally dawned on me that I couldn't become a conqueror unless I first had battles.

How blind I had been. After I accepted Jesus, I had been on the verge of a new beginning, but I failed to view the conflicts I was going through as golden opportunities to grow.

I had to accept the fact that as the days unfolded before me, I would be confronted with all sorts of good reasons to drink again, and each time I was faced with one of these reasons I had an opportunity to grow, but it depended on my decision. I could take my problem to God or try to handle it myself as before.

Drinking was still going to be a temptation for me when I had problems because it did offer a possible answer. I could hide my problems for awhile in a bottle. I had done this many times. That is what Satan is all about. Sin for a season can seem to resolve many problems, but the answers are, at best, temporary and the end result is always heartache. On the other hand I knew that God's answers offered me permanent solutions if that's what I wanted.

As before, Satan jumped in with both feet with his attacks against me. He wanted to keep me where I was and he started trying everything he possibly could to once again drive a wedge between me and God.

However, for the first time in my adult life, I was not afraid of the days ahead. My fears were gone as I sensed an excitement within me that I had never known before.

How beautiful it was to be fully assured and

confident that as I reached out for God's help, I would become more and more the conqueror that Jesus wanted me to be.

The answer had been there all the time and now, at last, I was ready to receive it. I had to make Jesus more than my Savior. He had to become my Lord. Jesus had to become more important to me than anything else in my entire life. I had to release everything to Him.

By now, all of my walls had been broken down. Not one was left standing. Yes, Jesus, I'm ready. This time, come all the way in!

Life More Abundantly

The entire restaurant seemed to go quiet and she just sat there staring at me. Even though it was our first date, I had looked her square in the eye and said, "Judi, I'm a recovered alcoholic. Would you like to go to church with me sometime.?"

For years, when I was still drinking, I had tried to make a deal with the Lord. I had a special prayer that usually went like this: "Oh Lord, you give me someone who I can love and who also loves me and I'll sober up."

Fortunately, in His Wisdom, He had never agreed to this prayer request because it would never have worked that way. God wanted me sober first. I had now been sober for almost a year and a half and I waited as patiently as I could for her answer.

At last the silence was broken and she said, "Yes." A few weeks later she told me that everything inside of her told her to slip quietly out the back door of the restaurant and run for her life. Since then, we have joked about this many times. As it turned out she didn't, and fourteen months later we were married.

From the beginning of our relationship, we started attending church together on a regular basis and it seemed that the more we went, the more we wanted to go. At first, we only went on Sundays, but soon we added a mid-week service. Then we decided to sign up for a New Believers Class.

It was here that we both began to experience on a first-hand basis the peace and joy manifested in John 10:10 where Jesus says, *"I have come to give you life and that more abundantly."*

Today it is easy for me to look back and understand what was happening in my life that affected it in such a traumatic way. Living as I was within a world of helplessness without God, I didn't need a reason to drink other than to temporarily escape from what I saw as meaningless existence.

"Bob, why do you drink the way you do?" I can't begin to recall the number of times I was asked this question. Never once could I honestly answer it. It wasn't that I had an answer that I wouldn't share. I simply didn't know why.

I once stated that my goal in life was not to run out of goals. I was always chasing something that I thought would bring me happiness, only to discover that once the goal was obtained, the elation that I experienced with my accomplishment was almost always immediately followed by a sense of emptiness knowing that I now had nothing to chase. My task then was to set up a new goal, and the race began all over again.

Clearly, something was wrong with the way I was looking at life. I believed that I had to be running all the time either toward or away from something. I tried handling my problems with the world's answers only to find that again and again they didn't work. The mere fact that I saw this pattern developing was in and of itself depressing.

Over the years, my belief had been that the more problem-free I could make my life, the more peace I could obtain. In the end, I realized that I was wrong. True peace is not the absence of problems. It is the ability to handle problems with God's help.

But God wanted all of me. He didn't want to share me with the world. Jesus had to be more than my Savior, He had to also be my Lord. Jesus needed to be in complete control of my life. When I finally threw my hands in the air and said, "Yes, Jesus, I'm ready. This time, come all the way in." It was then and only then that I began to experience the true peace that God had wanted me to have all along.

I began my new life by repeating a simple prayer that I had said several years before.

Dear Heavenly Father

I know that I am a sinner.
I believe that your son Jesus died on the
    cross for my sins.
I believe that He was raised on the third day
    from the dead and that He lives today.

I ask forgiveness for all of my past sins.
I am willing to turn away from all sin in my life.
Dear Jesus, I invite you into my heart as my personal Savior.
I ask that right now, you also become my Lord and help me daily to make your perfect will be done in my life.
In Jesus name I pray, Amen.

With this prayer I redicated my life to Jesus and my road to total recovery finally began. As I began learning how to apply God's answers to my problems, I found that His solutions were more than sufficient to carry me through. Seldom were God's answers the ones that I would have used before, but each time I overcame a problem with His help, I was strengthened. As my confidence and trust in God grew, it became easier and easier for me to turn over my new problems to Him as they arose. And with this I began to understand what true peace is all about.

Through prayer, reading the Bible, and fellowshipping with other believers, God had given me the tools to use to help me gain that permanent freedom from the bondage that alcohol had held me in for so long. However, it was my job to pick up these God-given tools and put them into use.

I once heard it said that God provides worms for the birds to eat, but He doesn't throw them into their nest. That made sense to me!

10

My Telephone To God

Through prayer, God had given me a direct line of communication to Him. Indeed, it was my own personal telephone to Heaven. Unfortunately, like many problem drinkers, I had seldom prayed except in times of emergency. "Oh Lord, help me get out of this mess! Help me get my job back! Help me with my court date! Oh Lord, please help me, and I'll never drink again!"

What a shock it had been when I realized that prayer was not my means of obligating God to help me get out of the messes I had created. Certainly, if all I had to do is pray everytime I got myself into trouble, the changes that God wanted to take place in my life would never happen.

Soon, my prayers began to take on a new direction and became more like this: "Oh Lord, help me to find out your plan for my life. Open the doors you want me to go through Lord, and give me the strength to close the doors behind me that you want closed."

At first, I was intimidated when I heard others praying, but as time went by, I came to realize that the length of my prayers and the exact words I used were unimportant. God was interested in what was in my heart, not my mouth.

Since then, some of the most beautiful prayers I have ever heard have come from children. These prayers are usually short, simple, and straight from the heart. I try to remember that we are all God's children. Some of us are just a little older.

The Lord's Prayer in Matthew 6:9-13 gave me a good example of how to structure my prayers. This didn't mean that I had to pray this way or God wouldn't listen; however, in the beginning it helped me develop my prayer life. I found that it was especially easy because it is broken into three parts.

The first part of the Lord's Prayer deals with my realizing whom I was praying to. *"Our Father in Heaven, Hallowed be Your Name."* I was praying to my Heavenly Father who was all powerful and everywhere. Genesis 1:1 says, *"In the beginning God created the Heavens and the Earth."* With this in mind, I had no doubt that He could help me with my drinking problem.

The second part of the Lord's Prayer involved my submission. *"Your kingdom come. Your will be done on Earth as it is in Heaven."* Not my will, but God's will had to become number one in my life. I would need His help in rearranging my priorities. This I knew would include people, places, and things.

The third part of the Lord's Prayer required

my asking for God's help in several areas. *"Give us this day our daily bread. And forgive us our debts, as we forgive our debtors. And do not lead us into temptation, but deliver us from the evil one."* God wanted me to come to Him with all my needs. They included necessities for life, forgiveness from sin, and deliverance from Satan's attacks.

At first this seemed like quite a bit for me to go through, but actually it wasn't. I found that I could acknowledge and worship God for who He was, ask for His will to be done in my life, and then bring before Him any specific needs I might have in a very short period of time.

Many times after a quick prayer, Satan would try to lay a guilt trip on me for praying for only a couple of minutes, but the Holy Spirit would remind me that prayer should be spontaneous and not restricted to special times and places. I could pick up my telephone to Heaven anytime and anywhere I wanted to. God was always open to what was in my heart.

Even though I knew I should start every morning and close every day with prayer, I also was aware that God wanted me to talk with Him when I was wide awake and alert. Since I am not always a "Springer" in the morning, many times it was necessary for me to wait until later so I could give Him good quality time.

For awhile, finding a time and place to pray in the middle of the day was a problem. During the week I was working and on weekends people were around and telephones and doorbells were ringing, but as I examined my schedule, I found that God helped me to set aside a special time to be alone with Him in private every single day. What a blessing it was to realize He was always there waiting for my call.

11

God's Telephone To Me

It has been said, "When all else fails, read the instructions." I can't think of a better application of this saying then when it comes to picking up God's instruction manual, the Bible, after everything else has failed. Certainly this was true in my case.

God had given me one of the most beautiful computers ever made. A brain. But if I had none of His answers stored away in my memory bank, when it came to a time of crisis, I had nothing to draw from. A computer can only punch out what's been keyed in.

I soon came to understand that all prayer should be coupled with the reading of God's Word. Just as prayer is my telephone to God, His Word, in the Bible, is His telephone to me. I Peter 2:2 advises that, *"as newborn babes, desire the pure milk of the Word, that you may grow thereby."*

In John 8:31-32, Jesus says, *If you abide in*

My Word, you are My disciples indeed. And you shall know the truth and the truth shall set you free."

I certainly was aware that I needed to read God's Word in order to both grow and to be set free from alcohol, but I had a problem. In the past when I had tried reading the Old King James version of the Bible, I had trouble understanding what it was saying.

When I found out that it had been written in the year 1611, I knew why I had experienced so much difficulty. Nearly four hundred years had passed since it had first been put into print and much of the language had changed.

Fortunately today, a totally up-to-date modern version of this same Bible is available. It is appropriately called the New King James Bible and after I saw it, I knew instantly that it was going to be easy for me to read and understand. This discovery became one of my major break-throughs, since I knew that God didn't want me guessing at what He was saying to me. Since that time I have also seen many other good up-to-date versions of the Bible that are available.

After my conversion in Memphis I had been told dozens of times to read the Bible, and start with the Gospel of John. In response to this, several times I picked up the Bible, but each time, instead of starting with the Gospel of John, I had begun in Genesis. The problem with this approach was that I was learning a lot about the history of Israel and refreshing my memory of many Sunday School stories, but I was not learning how to live my life today. Usually, by the time I got to Leviticus, I was drunk again.

I finally took the advice I had been given so many times and started with the Gospel of John. After I completed it, I continued through the New Testament until I had finished reading the book of Jude. It was in this section of the Bible, from the Gospel of John through Jude, that I found the answers that I had always wanted to know on how to deal with the guilt of all of my "yesterdays", how to cope with the fear of all of my "tomorrows", and how to obtain the peace I needed in order to make it through my "todays".

I read this one section of the New Testament many, many times before I was ready to move on to other parts of the Bible.

In the past, due to my eagerness to make up for lost time, I had read huge sections of the Bible every time I would sit down with it. Consequently, this required me to find large time slots when I could do this and this meant quite often I couldn't read every day. If I missed several days in a row, I would then begin promising myself that I would double or even triple up next time. This approach eventually would fail bringing about guilt for not following through and, ultimately, I would give up defeated.

This time I decided to limit my reading to two chapters a day but to make sure I read every day and it worked! In the long run this was far better than overwhelming myself and then burning out. Many days I had to force myself to stop, but I knew how easy it would be for me to fall into the old routine of overdoing it.

Just as I needed a physical cleansing

everyday, I also needed a spiritual cleansing everyday. Taking seven showers on Sunday morning wouldn't keep me clean all week. I found it was far better for me to read a little every single day and I was amazed at how great my days were going and also how much I was accomplishing.

As I read God's solutions in His Word and stored them away, I found continuing opportunities to use them. Many mornings after I had finished my reading, I thought I had really not gained much, but as time went on, it became apparent to me that I was recalling much more than I thought I was.

When problems arose, I now had a choice. I could use my old answers that I had used for years, which had never really worked, or I could use God's answers as I recalled them from my daily reading of His Word. This is how God spoke to me.

12

Free At Last

One of my biggest problems in the past, had been not being able to tell the difference between the voice of Satan and the voice of the Holy Spirit. At the same time that Satan was bombarding me with guilt, the Holy Spirit was also trying to talk with me, but I didn't know who was who. Distinguishing between the two voices could have been obvious to me a long time ago, but I had stayed confused because of my unwillingness to seek help.

What a blessing it was when I learned an easy test. If the voice was trying to put a wedge between God and me, the voice was coming from Satan. On the other hand, if the voice was telling me to repent and get closer to God I knew it was coming from the Holy Spirit. It was so simple. The Holy Spirit wanted to draw me closer to God, not push me away.

One of the most difficult of God's tools for me to put into practice was that of fellowshipping with other believers. For a time I tried to hang onto my old friends, but they simply didn't understand the new me. At best, what they would do is listen quietly while I shared with them what had happened to me, but usually as soon as they could, they would try to change the subject.

It also puzzled me at first why so many of my attempts to share Jesus with them turned into debates or even arguments. I discovered the reason in John 15:19 when Jesus taught His disciples, *"If you were of the world, the world would love it's own, Yet because you are not of the world, But I chose you out of the world, therefore the world hates you".*

At first it was extremely hard for me to reach out and meet new friends who were believers. For years one of my defenses had been to put on a false front.

Very few people had ever come to know the real Bob Lang because seldom would I let anyone get that close. Since I didn't like myself, I thought no one else could either.

Even people who had been around me during my problems only saw the end results of what I had done. Seldom would I reveal what had gone on inside of me prior to the crisis.

When anyone showed a special interest in me my conclusion was that what they truly liked was what I was doing or the false front that I was showing them.

With believers I knew I had to be open and honest and in the beginning I felt extremely vulnerable. However, I quickly discovered that they understood and accepted the new me, faults and all. It soon became exciting for me to share with them the changes that were taking place, and their continuing encouragement became one of the key factors in my growth.

For years, A.A. had been the only island of hope I had between court appearances and hospitals. In A.A. I had found refuge from the fear I constantly had of drinking again.

But now, through prayer, daily reading of the Word of God, and fellowshipping with believers, I gained more than a refuge. I gained that permanent means of escape from alcoholism that God had promised me in His Word in I Corinthians 10:13.

Today, drinking again is not even a passing thought. I still have problems. But now I bring them before the throne of God and He is always there to help, guide and comfort me.

Psalm 30:11-12 so vividly reminds me of how God has worked in my life so I could become one of His children forever and ever.

You have turned for me my mourning into dancing;
You have put off my sackcloth and clothed me with gladness,
To the end that my glory may sing praise to You and not be silent.
O LORD my God,
I will give thanks to You forever.

AUTHOR'S NOTE

Still sober! Still loving Jesus! It has now been over 40 years since my last drink in December of 1975. Our Heavenly Father through His Son Jesus has made a way of escape for me. What a blessing it is to know that His hand continues to reach out for others who are willing to take it and be truly free indeed!

Uncle Bobby's Finally Sober was first published in May 1987. Four months later the Billy Graham Evangelistic Association began using it with their source material and books for the next 24 years.

The year is now 2018 and over 40,000 copies are in circulation. This 77 page book has been widely used by multiple sources and is a quick read for those who need it.

May I personally assure you that our God loves you deeply and He is a God of mercy and grace! This book tells my story. It starts with pain and suffering but it ends with tears of joy. So can yours!

EPILOGUE

From 1980 until 1983 Bob served as the overseer of the Alcohol and Drug Recovery Program of Calvary Chapel in Costa Mesa, California. During that time, Bob's dream of teaching again was answered. He was offered an opportunity by Calvary Chapel to teach in their elementary school. With joy, Bob accepted that offer and taught 4th grade there for the next 22 years! Bob is now retired and living with his wife, Judi, in Arizona. Truly God restored to Bob the years that the locust had eaten.

Uncle Bobby has moved to Heaven!
August 1935 - January 2022

Praise God for His abundant love and mercy.

My Bobby was diagnosed
with dementia six years ago.
I am so grateful he did not have
to suffer a long illness.
He loved to make people laugh,
and he loved sharing his book.
Thank you for allowing me
to continue his ministry.
He was a wonderful man!

Judi Lang